## Big Machines

# DIGGERS

By Katie Kawa

**Gareth Stevens**
Publishing

**Please visit our website, www.garethstevens.com. For a free color catalog of all our high-quality books, call toll free 1-800-542-2595 or fax 1-877-542-2596.**

**Library of Congress Cataloging-in-Publication Data**

Kawa, Katie.
Diggers / Katie Kawa.
     p. cm. — (Big machines)
Includes index.
ISBN 978-1-4339-5560-0 (pbk.)
ISBN 978-1-4339-5561-7 (6-pack)
ISBN 978-1-4339-5558-7 (library binding)
1. Excavating machinery—Juvenile literature. I. Title.
TA735.K39 2011
621.8′65—dc22

                                        2011006571

First Edition

Published in 2012 by
**Gareth Stevens Publishing**
111 East 14th Street, Suite 349
New York, NY 10003

Editor: Katie Kawa
Designer: Daniel Hosek

Photo credits: Cover and all interior images Shutterstock.com.

Printed in the United States of America

CPSIA compliance information: Batch #CS11GS: For further information contact Gareth Stevens, New York, New York at 1-800-542-2595.

# Contents

Diggers make big holes.

A digger uses a tool to dig. It is called a bucket.

7

A digger has an arm.
This is called a stick.

A digger has a part called a house. A person can sit there.

The house moves!
It moves in a circle.

Diggers take down old homes.

Diggers move trees and dirt. Then, people make new homes.

One kind of digger is a backhoe. It has two parts.

A shovel is in the front.
A bucket is in the back.

The bucket has teeth.
The teeth cut rocks!

# Words to Know

bucket

shovel

# Index